Pushing thirty, wearing seventeen

Also by Melinda Smith and published by Ginninderra Press

Mapless in Underland

First… Then…

Melinda Smith

Pushing thirty, wearing seventeen

For Michael,
my family
and my sounding boards
Kirsten, Rosie and the Canberra Closet Poets 1998–99

Pusing thirty, wearing seventeen
ISBN 978 1 74027 083 0
Copyright © text Melinda Smith 2001
Copyright © cover design Catherine Swarbrick 2001

First published 2001
Reprinted 2015

Ginninderra Press
PO Box 3461 Port Adelaide SA 5015
www.ginninderrapress.com.au

Contents

Legends	7
Playing	9
Out of bounds	10
One brick wide	13
Dusk drive to Orange in the rain – the Cargo Road	16
Spring Street	18
Takoyaki II	20
The list	22
Sonnet for Mill Road	24
Parker	25
Spenser goes a-ravin'	27
Ballad of a chopped-up house	28
Blank verse bus journeys	30
Wake-up call	32
Thanks	35
Self-conscious haiku	36
Haiku from the Queanbeyan bus	37
Belconnen haiku	38
Three haiku	39
A passport for Frankie McLachlan	40
After the exam	42
Sonnet for M	43
Sister – 1	44
Sister – 2	45
Uncle Walt and the snowflakes	47
Last words	48
It's a front	49
Lines written on a bout of food poisoning	50
Chiasma	51
Zagreb niece	52
Tuol Sleng	53
Wedding sonnet	54

Legends

Rowdy, Chooka, Simmo, Roo,
PJ, Wardy, Macca too –
they strode the playground, bronzed and tall:
heroes, lions, legends all.

These boys, these men-to-be, had made
a very special kind of grade –
they'd cracked the footy hopeful's dream
and made the Western Region team,

a sacred brotherhood which brought
an immortality of sorts:
all those who had ascended thus
were fawned on by the rest of us.

Big Macca couldn't spell his name
but he was worshipped just the same,
and from the Senior Study portals
he dangled whimpering lesser mortals –

secure, his place as Chosen One
who walks forever in the sun,
never to be any less
than loved, and feared, and greatly blessed.

***

But, back then, none among us knew
that after passing singly through
the great white gate of graduation
old idols, starved of adulation,

thrown out alone, *sans* audience,
would never again seem so immense;
and age steals even the speed and skill
that made them kings of Footy hill.

Their immortality of sorts
a dusty file of sports reports.
Their path to greatness paved with tar:
the road to the job at the abattoir.

Oh, some went out in a blaze of glory,
legends right to the end of their story –
forestalling ignominious failure
in a howling scrum with a semi-trailer.

But most have suffered their god-like statures
to be shrunk to the sidelines of Sunday matches –
barracking fiercely for Dave and Bevan
in the mortal clash of the under-sevens.

Playing

'Where have you been, girl?'
'Over the road, Mum.'
'What do you *do* at the Fosters' all day?'
'Nothing, Mum, nothing…

>me and Sean Foster
>played doctors and nurses
>under the covers
>up in the top bunk
>under his red and blue
>racing-car sheet-set
>
>our thin, bony-shouldered
>gangly foal-bodies
>
>touching and smelling
>peering and feeling
>rubbing and humping…

nothing, Mum, nothing –
we were just playing.'

Out of bounds

They used to take us to be Physically Educated
up the tennis courts on Wednesday afternoons.
It was the furthest outpost, on the highest hill,
beyond the footy goalposts, on the boundary.

> We lugged the gear; tied back our hair.
> Our sweaty youth
> lunged back and forth
> bouncing on the concrete's glare.
>
> Above, the cemetery's stones
> rubbled the green
> we glimpsed between
> a shield of short and shaggy pines:
> forbidden turf, way out of bounds,
> where night-youth teased;
> drank; fondled; seized
> flesh-pleasures in the bone-filled grounds.
>
> Too young for those adventures, still,
> we vied to send
> our balls beyond
> the trees, onto the grave-crowned hill.
> Our tiptoe hope: to be allowed
> a brief trespass
> on secret grass;
> to penetrate the pine-tree shroud.
>
> Once, having begged Miss Miles, we slipped
> between the bars
> of iron. Not far
> into the search, we found a crypt.

We pushed our vital fingers in
to cracked cold stone.
The living bone
sang greeting to its buried twin,
and buried bone sang back, and told
of life's last day;
neglect; decay;
oblivion. Our hands went cold.

Palms charged with tingling secrets then,
We raised our heads.
The town was spread
below us, shimmering. (Look again).
The schools and homes began to fade,
the pubs; the shops;
the iron-clad tops
of churches blurred; roads were unmade,

till just the old volcano stood.
A double mound –
one thin, one round –
and shaggy-shouldered with thick wood.
It mocked us doubly with its lines:
the lean Young Man
the wide Old Man –
life's portrait sketched on a ridge of pines.
Yet mountain, out-enduring flesh
or mind or bone,
brick or gravestone,
laughs, and evades the cycle's mesh.

The vision flashed on tender brains:
we'd gazed full-face
on infinite space
whilst stood amongst our own remains.

We felt the danger then, and knew
why 'out of bounds'
fenced wrought-iron round
a graveyard with a mountain view.

One brick wide

At the old house in Summer Street
I'd challenge myself (on restless days)
to tightrope-walk the backyard fence.

The trick was never to look down –
the 'rope' was only one brick wide:
on the left the patchy green
of unkempt lawn, and on the right
the concrete glared. A thin brown line between,
no more. At six feet up, no net,
it was enough to spin your head
and make you chicken out. Not me…

Once, having inched the whole way round
to the final corner (at FULL height)
I faltered right at the tricky bit
where the gum tree branches thrust across
and tangled with your ankles. There
I had a little brush with life:

> I feel myself rock back. My head
> is light. My thoughts are floating oddly,
> going very slow. I sense
> the yawning air behind, the pull
> of gravity and concrete. This
> is it.

I wonder who will feed
the cat when I am gone, and who
will come across my broken-backed
remains jack-knifed across the drive.
They'll all be very sad. I see
my dad in black, supporting mum;
my brother (nursing heavy guilt
for never owning up about
the broken window they thrashed me for);
my teachers; all of 5A1 –
wishing they'd been nice to me
so they could sob 'I'll miss her' with
the right degree of sorrow to draw
sympathy and tenderness
from the captain of the footy team…

I watch my hands reach out toward
the blurry tree as it recedes
I think how nice it is to have
these gum leaves my last sight and breath
(much better than a car crash), though
I fear the pain of impact. Please
let my neck snap instantly,
I'll never feel a thing.

>   But then
> the flimsy single leaf I grasped
> with my slow-motion fingers *held*.
> I teetered back toward the tree,
> let go the leaf and dropped to hug
> the wall with all four limbs. Thank God.

We lived in that house for six more years
but I never walked the wall again.

Dusk drive to Orange in the rain – the Cargo Road

Coming home again for Dad's sixtieth
I leave the Canberra flat on a grey Saturday
to roll north through a thickening rain.

Hours later, as the car climbs the back of the tableland,
muddy water streams down the tattered road
and the potholes fill with milky tea.

Rags of cloud drift low over the orchards;
the town's dusk lights wink in the next valley;
the bruised sky blots the mountain out.

I remember it in different weather –
the fires that scorched the mountainside
and left it bald for years; the hail

that took the apple crop, but brought
a bumper year to every roofer,
set panel beaters up for life;

the snows that cut off the Sydney road;
the plague of mice out west.

                                          It's strange

but even after twelve years gone

I can open the Central Western Daily
and know a face on the wedding page
or turn to the In Memoriam

and recognise a name. They've been
here all this time – anchored, it seems
in trades; the abattoir; a child.

I, unencumbered, drifted off
to push my papers in another town.
I'll never live in this place again.

Perhaps, time come, I'll stay a month
to execute a will, and sell
the house – no more.

                                                                                                                  But every year

when the car drops down the last long hill
on the Cargo Road, and the home-made signs
shout 'CHERRIES FOR SALE' in red and white

it feels a lot like coming home.

Spring Street

One block long (and almost as wide)
the peeling houses and mangy lawns
faced each other all down the road:
a workers' parade of 'semi-detacheds'.

At one end, like a mislaid chunk
of ancient wedding cake, still sat
the town's first Council Chambers (sunk
by then to the status of Sunday School).

From there to the cheapie patho-lab
behind steel bars at the other end
was property of the Spring Street Mob:
our one-road realm all afternoon.

> There were the Brewers, who, if you 'crawled'
> would let you go on their slip'n'slide
> all the way down their muddy backyard
> in the merciless summer holidays;
>
> and 'no-bath' Mick, with snot-nosed sisters
> sporting rag-doll hair; and Kim
> who got the trampoline for Christmas
> and split her head on Boxing Day;
>
> and the Snells, who everybody knew
> were far too closely interbred
> (each year a wobbly girl or two
> would pop out a child to her brother or dad).

> We used to have raucous games of cricket
> – the 'our end' kids against the rest –
> with no 'LB', and a steel bin wicket.
> Any front yard was six and out.
>
> I remember the time the boys got caught
> exploding the Henessys' letterbox.
> The flames had leapt to fourteen feet
> (or so the ropable mother claimed).
>
> My brother said 'Bullshit!' (Lord preserve us –
> he said it that way to the cops as well).
> He still got off with community service
> (always *could* dodge what was coming to him).

But we don't own it any more –
the homes have lost the families
they held; the yards fenced in; new doors;
and one or two 'done up'. Who knows

the paths of all those countless Snells?
There's none here now. The vacant block
has sprouted flats. A bright sign sells
them: 'Home for Confused Elderly'.

Takoyaki II

(Osaka, Autumn 1992)

I brought you a hot and fragrant gift
– carried it muffled against the cold
the seven blocks from Senri East –
a dozen takoyaki balls
in a box of squeaky styrofoam.

You met me at the door, and took
the box with gentle hands. You smiled.
The smell enveloped both of us
and rushed from under the opened lid
to fill your tiny room. The dumplings
glistened under sticky sauce
and seaweed shards. We breathed the steam
in long delicious lungfuls, knelt
and started in. I sank my teeth
into my first, then whistled air
to cool my heat-numbed lips. You laughed
and watched me as I ate. Your eyes
were soy-brown, rice-white question marks.

I rolled a mouthful round my tongue,
feeling the chafe of the crispy skin.
The chunks of baby octopus
inside, firm nuggets in the soft
and slippery batter. Mmmm. I smiled
my answer back at you across
the low kotatsu table. Yes.

Eyes locked, we polished off the lot,
and licked the last of stickiness
from salty fingers.

                        Afterwards

a whiff of takoyaki steam
would always thrust your memory
in front of every other thought
of mine, so real I could have sworn
you knelt before me.

                        What a feast.

The list

I watched the news and the newsreader cried:
huge fat droplets, magnified
by his black-rimmed Japanese glasses.

I watched some more, as the newsreader read
from a list (reproduced behind his head)
of handwritten names and ages:

> '…Noda Hanako, age 79
> Ikeda Koji, age 26
> Tanaka Mayumi, age 7…'

Quietly, the newsreader cried
on. Gulping water, he paused, and tried
(and failed) to regulate his breathing.

One by one, the newsreader read
five thousand names confirmed as dead
on the morning after the earthquake:

> '…Kinoshita Jun, age 16
> Moriuchi Naoko, age 43
> Kimura Masaaki, age 65…'

I don't know for sure why the newsreader cried –
perhaps he knew someone who had died
(quite likely if he was local)

> '…Hisamaru Sen, age 52
> Noguchi Keiko, age 89
> Arajima Miharu, age 31…'

Or perhaps, the newsreader thought, as he read
of the grief in every name he said
for each of the watching families:

> '…Matsuda Shinji, age 4
> Aoyama Yuko, age 15
> Sato Akira, age 22…'

But I think the newsreader thought, as he cried
(as each of us would, down dark inside)
dear god, what if that had been me?

> 'Melinda Smith, age 29.'

Sonnet for Mill Road

No nature strips, no fortress lawns defend
or shield the dwellings from their neighbourhood:
our scanty walls are shared, like scraps of food
among the grizzled, reeking-suited men
of City Park; our doors all scrape a street
that brawls with midnight life. And all the mail
thrust early through the hole, not left to stale
decay in far off, boxed, hedge-buried heat.

Our unsuburban road no cul-de-sac,
but main arterial: thick-flowing, hot,
and death to cut across. Quick-trafficked flood:
no tourniquet above the needle track –
no safe chicanes to form a calming clot
or pool, in Crescent Billabongs, dead blood.

Parker

(Cambridge 1996)

I live here
at the centre.
This is my turf.
I can see it all with my four elevated faces:
my domain marked out in diamonds;
bordered with trees;
open to the wind.

You pass through
(most of you) –
some quickly, humming past on shining metal;
some squeaking on worn leather, mudguards racketing;
or hulking with distended rustling bags:
heads down, eyes forward, gaze horizon-bound
and never seeing me.

Those who stay
are temporary:
blotching the parched grass with red and white bare bodies;
ambling to and fro in mystic white-clad dances, red balls flying;
pairing up on windy days to raise a kite up level with my
eye.
And on summer evenings you flock, the young ones,
bikes circled like wagons against discovery.
Within, you talk and drink and fondle uninhibited –
but I see you.

Even these long visits end – your stumps are upped,
your kites are crashed, your bodies burned, your journey over.
Yet here I stay, deep-rooted,
still, and waiting.

At night when you are gone I throw out a great circle –
light with four centres.
When the snow comes the ground is a luminous plain
and I am its sun.
When the mist comes my circle shrinks
until only I exist.

My huge vision contracts to my own long body:
the peeling paint and cast iron ridges
modulating at my ankles into sculpted fish;
my four globes illuminating only
the glassy crumbs that twinkle on the grey
around my great, square
foot.

It is I,
Parker,
and this is my Piece.

Spenser goes a-ravin'

(For G. Francis Dunford)

It happened on a humming May midnight:
We chipped through London's streets of gritted teeth,
shoving the hard-faced crowds. We fought to breathe.
Heat spilled from sources doorwayed out of sight.
Sound and pulse and light
came strobing through a hard, black-cornered chink
and pulled us all across a threshold there
(although we rocked and twittered on the brink)
and thrust us into caves of beating air
and sweating rainbows, where
a hundred London faces liquefied,
their lips unstiffened, joyful mouths howled wide
in songs and kisses, secrets welling out
with love in frantic floods.
                            But midnight tide

peaks, turns and rushes out –
so dawn's return of doubt
drained dry the drenching chambers; slammed their doors;
left untongued secrets clenched in firm-set jaws.

Ballad of a chopped-up house

(with apologies to Philip Larkin and A.A. Milne)

I am a room in a chopped-up house
(in a five-bed, no-lounge, chopped-up house)
and there once was a lady lived in me
was as far round the bend as she could be –
but was fine, far as anyone else could see –
in a chopped-up house in Cambridge.

She dragged every day to her fucked-up job
and she moaned home again from her fucked-up job.
She peeled off her days like sweat-soaked clothes
and she piled them in corners and piled them in rows –
unwashed, unexamined, and on the nose,
in a chopped-up house in Cambridge.

Bits of meals she dredged from the cramped-up stove;
and the grease-caked pots from the cramped-up stove;
and last month's news, and the month's before;
all mulching down on my mouldering floor,
with her piled days pushing against the door
of her locked-up room in Cambridge.

Still she shoved through my knee-deep, choked-up space –
through her days, unreclaimed, in my choked–up space.
Her bed was a pile of unopened mail
and her dreams were of soapies, and telesales,
and a dim understanding going stale
in a chopped-up house in Cambridge.

And then one day, in the chopped-up house,
she stopped dragging out to her fucked-up job.
The house-mates thought it was slightly queer
but did nothing (discreetly) for over a year –
not till the rot-stench and rats appeared
in the chopped-up house in Cambridge.

When the landlord forced through my locked-up door
she was festering there on my fouled-up floor:
dwarfed by her heaped-up life's debris;
overcome by the fumes of her lethargy.
She'd been fine – far as anyone else could see –
in a chopped-up house in Cambridge.

Blank verse bus journeys

They warned me not to travel on the bus:
'They're full of loonies, love!' But all I saw,
at 8.15, were Monday's silent suits –
crammed close, embarrassed, eyes avoiding eyes,
resisting hard the rolling impetus
of rhythm's wheels, grim clinging to the poles
as if to sanity, afraid to touch
or brush, unwitting, any body else.

The warned-of ones I met much later on,
long after suits had disembarked, desk-bound.
Some manic soul would shuffle on, and sit;
would find my eyes, and rave about his son,
or hold my hand, or laugh, or scream, or plead.
I felt no threat – was sometimes quite amused:
one woman sang, her head lolled upside down,
inverted throat awail with lullabies.

Such were the 'loonies' – harmless (so I thought) –
until the Monday bus was stormed by one.

He galloped down the silent aisle, and laughed
in startled faces, drawn despite themselves
to meet his eyes, and then he wheeled and cried
'Cheer up, youse bastards! Right, let's hear youse sing!'
He led off with a chorus, voice wind-wild
and howling through the still uneasy space:
'Now you join in!' he ordered, growling close.
We felt the pull of madness, cleared our throats

and launched into *Come All Ye Faithful* – faint
at first, but swelling by the second verse
to wake deep-slumbered feeling, drown our doubt
and make a unison of eyes and smiles.
And for a full ten minutes we regained
our sense of joining full with fellow fools
to forge a larger thing. We loosed our holds
on straps and poles – forgot to be afraid.

And even after getting off, dispersing
in shrugged bemusement, into separate days,
a feeling stayed with each, a vertigo:
the cliff's-edge rush of souls, unhusked, communing.

Wake-up call

It's Tuesday morning. Six a.m.
A faint grey light between the blinds.
The voices in the radio
announce the news, and I recoil.
I burrow under all the sheets.
The weatherman persists, his words
still filter through my tight cocoon.

And then, I hear another voice
behind the *isolated showers* –
a man – or lots of men? – far off.
It sounds like footy training. Seems
a little early in the day
for all that bellowing and sweat…

I wonder if downstairs can hear
(she carps at out-of-hours noise).
The radio fades out. Outside
the sounds are clearer now, and close
below the window – just one voice.
I can make out words and moans:

> WAAAKE UUUP!!!!
> Youse fucken soft-cocks
> WAAAKE UUUP!!!
> I'll fucken kill the lot of youse
> Come out, youse cunts
> I'll take youse all fucken on
>
> Where AAARE You???!

WHERE AARRE YOU ??!!

WHERE
AARRRE
YOOOOUUUU?!!!

The echoes bounce off all the flats
that face the hollow atrium.
I twitch the curtains open, and
peer out – there's no-one there. I try
the other windows – not a glimpse
of our accuser, though his voice
still shakes the walls – *WAAAKE UUP YOUSE CUNTS*

The Yellow Pages…*P…P…P…*
Police Attendance. Someone bored
picks up the phone: 'Location please.'
I start, but then he interrupts.
'Yeah, unidentified young male
at Murdoch Street, we've been informed –

car's on its way.' I thank him, then…
it seems there's nothing to left to say
so I hang up. I pace the cold,
tiled kitchen floor in search of food.
Outside, he's still in violent voice:
Youse fucken soft-cocks, come on out

I flinch, then try to concentrate
on toast and coffee, thumping round
the drawers and cupboards in a fit
of sudden energy. And yet
the half a loaf that I devour
leaves me unsatisfied. Outside

the voice has lowered – just a few
defensive mutters. Others, now,
are firing questions, barking orders –
circling round the first. The cops
have come. I strain to see the car
but even that's invisible.

And then, the voices all recede
and cease. Silence returns. I stand
and stare at nothing for a while.
Seems like it's over then – the threat
located, muzzled, neutralised,
and me still in my slippers. Strange –

I should be grateful, I suppose –
no hand-to-hand ordeal, no fuss,
the inconvenience removed,
like mess from offices, dispatched
while most of us are still asleep
by unseen hands. Why so surprised –
what other end did I expect?

Thanks

To sit;
>to feel the autumn sun

hug my back like a tender friend;

to taste fresh semolina cake –
solid, sticky, nutty-warm;

to watch a shower of yellow leaves
tumble to the quivering grass;

to be alone with paper, pen,
imagination, time –
>a gift.

I didn't notice at the time
but let me thank you anyway.

Self-conscious haiku

She laughs (too loudly).
More champagne. Pushing thirty,
wearing seventeen.

Haiku from the Queanbeyan bus

One

In the wilting heat
vinyl bus seats run with sweat;
the long road shimmers.

Two

Bushy green poplars
stand like happy squirrels' tails
brushing the blue sky

Belconnen haiku

One

Huge squat office blocks
glare at delicate gum trees
like alien ships.

Two

The afternoon clouds:
white smudges from floury hands
on a sky-blue cloth.

Three

Ghost gum trunks flit past –
the hill's bleached skeleton shows
under bunched green fur.

Four

The winter sun sets
like a lone light winking out
at the earth's cold edge.

Five

All night on the road:
a thin grey conveyor belt
moves from dark to dark.

Three haiku

Spring in the vines

New green tendrils coil
towards each other, trembling,
eager buds erect.

Leftover Olympic figure

This gaudy statue –
body a wafer of tin –
has great, concrete feet.

Long journey

His father rocks him,
safe in the crook of an arm:
speechless tenderness.

A passport for Frankie McLachlan

(For all the euro-lemmings)

This document entitles him who carries it to pass
without a let or hindrance, over sea and over land.
May the bearer be protected – though his ready cash be sparse,
and connections non-existent – by a special helping hand.

So if you're old, with rancid breath, and into model trains
and your seat is next to Frankie's on a sixteen-hour flight:
may you find you've suddenly become allergic to all planes
and may he use your vacant seat to stretch out for the night.

And if you walk behind him with a pen-knife in your hand,
reaching up to slash his backpack in the middle of a crowd:
may you trip before you get there, somersault, and when you land
find your knife stuck in your buttock, and him laughing rather loud.

If you're a tiny microbe with a laxative effect
who's swimming round in Frankie's steaming bowl of Tom Yum Goong:
may his chopsticks catapult you and deposit you direct
on the plate of that Victorian who called the chef a boong.

And if you're a London geezer who sells Lachie little pills
wot are made of Rid and Omo (though you call them 'ecstasy'):
may he lose his little purchase 'ere they do him any ill
and may you swallow some, and wake up mentally aged three.

As for the drunken football team, out, after a defeat
who tries to tear him limb from limb for being in the way:
may the other team, and all its fans, appear across the street
and lay in with their iron pipes as Frankie slips away.

And so it goes for all the hazards Lachie-boy may meet:
Pamplona bulls and Damart thieves and even Scrumpy Jack.
From the bouffy hair upon his head to the RM's on his feet
may he always be protected – may he one day make it back.

After the exam

Sick waves of stale adrenalin
twist up the guts; the head is thick
with last night's load of crammed-in waste;
and spasms twitch the raw-gnawed fingers,
stained with blue. The heart has aged from pounding;
eyes have strained and lost
another several seeing hours;

and on the soul, a further scar:
the stripes left by a barcode scan –
the latest in a series, like
a prisoner's tally of his days:
a row of marks on a cold stone wall.

Sonnet for M

When first we met, you never gave me cause
to doubt that I would leave you far behind
as other loves; that parting was no pause
but ending to our bond – and now I find
that parted once, and twice, we still endure
inseparable, and that which I mistook
for light short story, meriting no more
than six-month's space of blanks in last year's book,
has grown into a sprawling trilogy:
on three years' calendars now hangs the tale,
in each a fine reunion scene. And we,
page-turning yet, love on, on epic scale.
        So far, then, guessed I wrong: then would I fill
        the shelves with such mistakes, and make them still.

Sister – 1

Who would have thought
you'd be going down
the aisle of the old church
twice in the space of a month ?

The first time
        you made your proud advance
        in your new white shoes
        all the way to the altar.

The second time
        they had to carry you.

It was so soon
they could almost have used the same flowers.

And all the same faces
whose eyes were dabbed with hankies
on your wedding day

reappeared a fortnight later
with their raw grief streaming
down their disbelieving cheeks.

Sister – 2

When you left us like that
it felt like a cyclone
had ripped the roof from the house.

The rest of us clung to furniture,
hands out to each other,
bewildered by the violent sky that yawned above the living room.

When you left us like that
I thought the dark rain
would lash our upturned faces forever.

***

Nobody told me
you'd flit back at odd moments
in the damp, splintered calm of afterwards.

Like a trick of the light
bringing back the old carpet
to the stripped floorboards;

like a strange echo
blaring a ten-year-old song
from a dead radio.

Nobody told me
I'd be taking up smoking,
remaking that air
you always had with you.

But I knew for sure
I would never lose you
when you came to me in a dream

saying wake up you
go and look
at your new house.

Uncle Walt and the snowflakes

Reading Uncle Walt by my window:
> *The white-topt mountains show in the distance, I fling out my fancies toward them.*

I blink among the snow feathers
as they meet and part, chase and flee each other.

I can not tell who leads or follows
in the grey soft downward-milling

but my eyes fix on the ones blown upward –
improbable heroic tufts,
they float before me
distinct, triumphant;
describe their unique arc and fall

to join the others on the ground.
And yet I mark them as they go:
> *I understand the large hearts of heroes.*

Last words

Here am I in a five-day grind
with a two-day sleep at either end,
thinking vaguely of my old friend
and I look about myself to find

I can't recall your married name
or where it is you're living now.

Time was I thought I'd always have
the daily comfort of your face.

> I saw you last at that hurried meal
> before my trip four years ago
> when, in a fog of hugged goodbyes
> we muttered words like 'love' and 'miss'

I never meant that as the end.
I got distracted for a while

and now I've let it go so long
you might as well be dead (or me?)

> Our last words to each other were:
> 'We'll write, won't we?' – 'Yes, we must.'

It's a front

You think you know me?
You think you love me?
You can't know me, you terrify me
You can't love me, I'm not here

I'm foetus-curled and whimpering behind this tall facade:
a life-size cardboard doll that moves and speaks
but doesn't show a fucking thing I really think.
And now you've gone and touched your mouth to her cardboard cheek
and poured your passion in her cardboard ears,
I'll have to stay right where I am
and leave this cardboard love affair to run its course
without a word from me…
Best wishes to you both –
I hope she's stiff 'n' shiny long enough to last it out – I'm thinking
six months at the most
before she starts to sag,
me sweating all the while to prop her up.
I hope
you do eventually catch on –
I'd hate to end up trapped back here
to eavesdrop on a drawn-out game of happy families,
or, even worse, to finish
mute and helpless
pinned beneath
a cardboard coffin lid…

Lines written on a bout of food poisoning

Nausea spasmed its shuddering way
up my innocent spine; one juddering punch
in the guts and I lost it: my dignity sprayed
on the door of the toilet, along with my lunch.

The rest of the night my intestines and I
held a battle of wills. I began to give in.
'Take this bucket of suffering from me,' I cried
through my sick dizzy fog. My brain doubled its spin.

My body, my temple? Relentless; possessed.
Like some violent elimination machine,
it retched, purged and drained me of all I had. Rest
only came when exhaustion had knocked me out clean.

I revived within twenty-four hours. I mused
on my recent ordeal. One thought turned me cold:
I woke up from the nightmare – when body refused
all directives of will –

                        but I won't when I'm old.

Chiasma

My father
lies wheezing.
His heart blood
has halted.
The bedroom
I enter
in sorrow
has altered.

Wrought on
by weeping,
I flee
from bedchamber;
from the stopping
at the core
of my blue-lipped
young father.

Zagreb niece

You were hours old when I heard the news
in a bleary pre-dawn telephone call:
a lion heart who wouldn't lose;
a *caesar* after twelve hours' strain.

I thought of the hard midsummer night
you and your mother must have had:
you burrowing gutsily out to the light,
she giving her stubborn womb up to be cut –

with visions of your bewildered dad
pacing a foreign hospital ward
while foreign doctors held all he had
in foreign hands, at a scalpel's edge –

while several continents away
we willed the telephone to ring,
shivering on that icy day,
fearing the worst, with our mouths shut tight.

Tuol Sleng

(former Khmer Rouge prison S21)

Last night I saw a hundred thousand skulls
behind my eyes – whole villages of bones
reached for me, jawing wordless moans.
Last night I dreamed a hundred thousand skulls

but yesterday I walked a tranquil beach
and swam at sunset in a pearl-green sea.
The tide drained all my thoughts away from me,
beyond the fishing nets and out of reach.

> Two weeks ago I toured a prison's shell:
> five years of victim's pictures stared at me
> from silent walls – a murder gallery.
> Two weeks ago I walked the halls of hell.
>
> That night I felt warm breezes in my dreams;
> ate fresh mango by sparkling waters; heard
> wet children laughing as the palm fronds stirred.

Last night I heard a hundred thousand screams.

Wedding sonnet

I'll never shed a new light upon 'love' –
my weeks of feeble flickering outshone
by centuries of flaming words upon
bright pages. Over and above
that fire, I have one tiny spark to cast,
and that's to testify the truth of this:
the joy limelit by all those songs, that bliss,
you give to me each day, from first to last.

Today we marry, bathed both in that glow.
Today we marry, and tonight we leave
this smiling ring of lights, and inch away
to dimmer places fewer torches know
along a winding path. But I believe
two candles are enough to light the way.

www.ingramcontent.com/pod-product-compliance
Lightning Source LLC
Chambersburg PA
CBHW062204100526
44589CB00014B/1945